Can You Sing?

sing

jump

dance

run

read

write

swim

fly

Can you sing?

Yes. I can sing.

Can you jump?

Yes. I can jump.

Can you dance?

Yes. I can dance.

Can you run?

Yes. I can run.

Can you swim?

Yes. I can swim.

Can you fly?

No, I can't.

Let's learn about
the United Kingdom (UK).

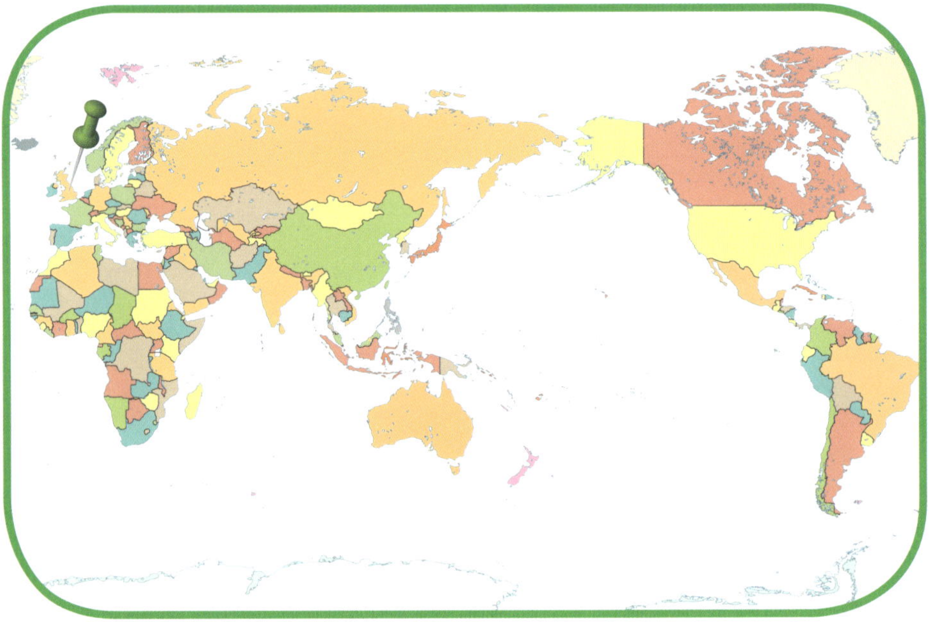

Flag of UK
(Union Jack)

Big Ben